DUPLE THE DOMINANT ERA

Howard Berry

First published 2024

Amberley Publishing
The Hill, Stroud
Gloucestershire, GL5 4EP

www.amberley-books.com

ISBN 978 1 4456 8682 0 (print)
ISBN 978 1 4456 8683 7 (ebook)

British Library Cataloguing in Publication Data.
A catalogue record for this book is available from the British Library.

Origination by Amberley Publishing.
Printed in the UK.

Contents

Introduction

Over the years, several excellent books have been produced documenting in great detail the history of Duple, and these have been invaluable in assisting with historical information for this publication. I don't intend to try and emulate the depth of information provided in those most illustrious tomes, but rather provide a potted history of the company and then showcase its products through the pictures and comments which make up the body of this book. Those of you who have read my previous books will know that I have little interest in the faceless boxes of today, much preferring vehicles manufactured during the 1970s and 1980s, the era of my misspent youth, and so making the content of this book fit into that timescale means I can go right up to the end of Duple production without also having to (with great relief) navigate through the minefield of body styles that the company appeared to produce during the 1960s.

But first, back to how it all began. The dictionary defines the word duple as something having two parts – double; twofold – and in 1919, Herbert White formed Duple Bodies and Motors in Hornsey, London, having previously built a dual-purpose vehicle under the Bifort name at premises in Farnham, Hampshire. These were former military Ford Model Ts fitted with bodies that looked like a small car but could be transformed into a van by removing the rear portion and fitting a van-type roof. Obviously, such a vehicle was ideal for the owner of a small transportation business, who could have both a private hire vehicle and goods carrier all in one. The product range was further enhanced by the introduction of a pick-up, as well as a version with slide-out display shelves. Such was the popularity of these bodies that, in 1926, a new factory was opened in Hendon. The company had also dabbled in building coachwork and 1928 saw the company decide to concentrate on this and production of the dual-purpose bodies was discontinued. This turned out to be a good move as within ten years the factory employed upwards of 750 staff and, in 1928, Walter Brown, a former partner in the Strachan & Brown bodybuilding business, joined Duple and subsequently had a major influence on the company's future expansion.

The 1930s was a decade of expansion for Duple, with not only large orders coming in from the home market, but export orders were also on the increase thanks mainly to the hard work put in by Walter Brown, and this helped to compensate for the seasonal reductions in UK orders. Business overall however was booming, and in 1934 the original factory was extended by the purchase of 3½ acres of land adjoining the current site. One significant event that took place in 1931 was the announcement by Bedford of two passenger chassis (the fourteen-seat WHB and twenty-seat WLB) and Duple became one of the four bodybuilders recommended by Bedford, leading to a close association that would last for over fifty years until the demise of both Bedford and Duple.

In 1946 the name of the business was changed to Duple Motor Bodies Limited and post-war production commenced with the introduction of what is probably Britain's most iconic vehicle, the Duple Vista-bodied Bedford OB. When combined with rebodies built on pre-war chassis, Duple's order book was filled for several years ahead, these bodies tending to be metal-framed, partly due to their greater durability and partly because of a shortage of timber for traditional bodywork. The post-war boom was not to last long, however, and a rapid decline in orders in the 1950s resulted in a difficult time for the bodybuilding industry in general. Duple also suffered more than others due to a nine-month strike, which resulted in such a catastrophic loss of business that the company seriously considered moving out of London. This move could have been easily achieved with the purchase of Nudd Brothers & Lockyer Limited in 1952, based in Kegworth, and the acquisition of premises in Loughborough in 1955, which resulted in 1956 in the formation of Duple Motor Bodies (Midland) Limited. In 1958, Willowbrook of Loughborough was also acquired and operated as a separate subsidiary until sold in 1971. A further takeover that was pivotal in Duple's history was the 1960 purchase of H. V. Burlingham, of Blackpool. Whilst this initially added a northern arm to Duple's production (the factory being renamed Duple Motor Bodies (Northern) Limited in 1962), in 1968 it was decided to transfer all coach production to Blackpool, and two years later the Hendon factory was closed. Shortly afterwards, Duple was sold to Frank Ford, an entrepreneur in the coaching world, and George Hughes from private investment company Capitarium with Herbert White remaining as president of the company.

In 1961, Duple introduced the well-known Bella range of bodies for fitting onto Bedford chassis, which consisted of the Bella Vista (for the Bedford VAS), Bella Vega (Bedford SB range) and Bella Venture (Bedford VAM). When the maximum permitted length for coaches was increased to 36 feet and the maximum width to 8 feet 2½ inches, Duple (Northern) produced the Continental for fitting onto heavyweight chassis such as the AEC Reliance and Leyland Leopard, and there can't be many bus-mad children of a certain age who didn't have the Dinky model of the Vega Major-bodied Bedford VAL. Duple saw the 1960s out with the Commander and the Viceroy, the latter replacing the majority of the Bella range.

The first two years of the 1970s saw Willowbrook sold to George Hughes, Herbert White (the company's founder) pass away, and Duple itself sold to the Cranleigh Group, a Manchester-based industrial holdings company with Frank Ford remaining as Executive Chairman. The 1972 Commercial Motor Show saw the launch of the new Dominant range, which, together with the Panorama Elite and Supreme from the UK's other main coachbuilder, Plaxton, were to be the mainstay of British coaching throughout the 1970s, and apart from a smattering of bodies from Willowbrook, Portuguese coachbuilder Salvador Caetano and a little-known Belgian concern named Van Hool (wonder what happened to them?), there was very little competition. All this, however, was to change, and not for the better.

The Transport Act of 1980 saw the deregulation of coach services over 30 miles in length and several high-profile (and some not so high) operators started to operate inter-city coach service in competition with the (then) state-owned National Express. The early 1980s also saw a huge surge in the Continental holiday shuttle market, and passengers travelling on these very long-distance services – in some cases for days on end – quite rightly deserved greater levels of comfort than had hitherto been known. Operators suddenly needed to look for high-specification coaches to get the edge over their competitors and keep their passengers happy, and features such as reclining seats, toilets, on-board catering facilities and entertainment systems became the required norm rather than the exception. Neither Duple nor Plaxton had vehicles with these facilities as standard, but the foreign bodybuilders did – and soon the floodgates opened. By the end of 1982, the market was awash with high-floor executive specification coaches of Continental manufacture. To compete with them, the Dominant (and its high-floor sibling, the Goldliner) were replaced by two new designs, the Laser and the Caribbean, but these did little to halt the slide in production. To put this into perspective, Duple's output fell from 1,000 bodies in 1976 to 800 in 1980, and to just over 500 in 1981. A year later, output was just 340 bodies.

In 1983, Duple was sold to the Hestair Group and renamed Hestair Duple. Hestair already owned Guildford-based Dennis and in 1987 the group announced a new integral coach built with a Duple body and Dennis running units. Named the Duple 425 (after its drag coefficient of 0.425, which made it the most aerodynamic coach on the market at the time), its initial popularity wasn't enough to boost the order book and the business continued to struggle. By 1988, Duple's output was just 250 bodies. In November 1988, Hestair announced that they were selling the Dennis and Duple businesses to a management buyout team, operating under the name Trinity Holdings with the company being renamed Duple International. However, this was to be short-lived, and in July 1989 the decision was made to close the Duple operation. The jigs for some of the current range, including the 425 integral and Duple Services Ltd, the spares and repair business, were purchased by Duple's long-time UK rival, Plaxton of Scarborough. Thus ended seventy years of Duple Motor Bodies Limited.

As with my other books, the photographs are taken when the coaches were in service so as to evoke memories from the time, whether it be the cars, the people and their fashions or just the locations. This book does contain rally shots, not the rallies of today, but the coach rallies of the 1970s and 1980s, events where manufacturers showcased their new products and operators showed off their new flagships. As usual, I have been greatly assisted in my endeavours by a handful of photographers to whom I am indebted, not only for letting me use their work, but also for having the foresight to record these vehicles in their heyday for others to enjoy so many years later. Each photographer has an initialled credit after their work: Alan Snatt (AS), Martyn Hearson (MH), Richard Simons (RS) and Paul Green (PG). Finally, in order to reduce the word count, NBC refers to the National Bus Company, SBG the Scottish Bus Group, VCS to London Victoria coach station and the Leopard and Tiger are products of the Leyland zoo.

Howard Berry, Cheswardine

Dominant

Introduced in 1972 and launched at that year's Commercial Motor Show, the Dominant was Duple's first body design built with an all-steel structure and, despite being replaced as the company's full-sized body by the Laser and Caribbean in 1983, was to remain in production until 1985, the final two years seeing the body remain available for fitting to the Bedford SB and VAS. The Dominant was a direct assault on the Plaxton Panorama Elite, a model that was making Duple's current range look distinctly ancient. The Dominant had deep single-piece windows with narrow pillars between them, below which was a deep ribbed chrome strip running the length of the body. Both the front and rear screens were gently curved and were level with the side windows, with the front end being finished by twin headlights either side of a barred central grille. Illuminated destination displays or name panels could either be fitted in the grille area or in a dome above the windscreen.

The Dominant became an instant success. Some of the country's most prominent fleets took large numbers and the newly formed National Bus Company placed substantial orders too, the Dominant-bodied Leyland Leopard becoming the standard coach in many of the NBC's subsidiaries. The Dominant was also available in express form, whereby it was fitted with two-piece entrance doors leading to a wide platform and was fitted with destination equipment as well as facilities for fitting a ticket machine. When built to this configuration it became eligible for the government's Bus Grant scheme, whereby operators were able to buy a coach with a substantial grant provided most of its early life was spent on stage carriage operations.

Unusual versions of the Dominant were a batch of bodies fitted to Leyland Leopard chassis for Nottingham City Transport. Fitted with bus seats, no forced air ventilation and devoid of any external brightwork, the model was known as the Dominant E-type. The year 1975 saw another unusual vehicle hit the roads of Britain, namely the Dominant Goldliner. Built as a collaboration between Bedford and Duple as a Bedford demonstrator, the Bedford YMT chassis featured a more powerful 8.2-litre version of Bedford's 500 series engine, and the Dominant body was fitted with a higher floor than normal. The coach was taken to Marrakesh to see how it fared when being driven in a hot climate and over terrain in various states of disrepair. The concept remained just that and the coach returned to the UK where it was retained by Bedford but spent its days running initially in NBC National white livery before being used by Tricentrol of Dunstable. It remained unique in the UK but there were also two Goldliners built on left-hand drive Volvo B58 chassis for export.

Well, the first picture of the book might as well be of a first! Wilder (Golden Miller) of Feltham's MYV 792L was the first Duple-bodied Volvo to be delivered and only the second Volvo to be delivered new to a UK operator. A 1973 B58, it is seen taking part in that year's Brighton Coach Rally, the relaxed driver with a cigarette in his mouth unaware he's got a boy racer in a Mk 1 Escort up his rear. (AS)

Another operator taking the plunge with the new body/chassis combination of Volvo and Dominant was Skill's of Nottingham, who took delivery of two identical vehicles in June 1973. The first of the pair was FTV 10L, seen in Newcastle-under-Lyme. (AS)

Nowadays, most coaches in my home county of Shropshire are operated either directly or by subsidiary companies of Lakeside of Ellesmere, but back in the 1970s there were several sizeable concerns in the county. The closest to me would have been Salopia of Whitchurch, whose fleet was predominantly lightweight chassis such as Bedford and Ford. Dominant-bodied CNT 315L was one of the latter and was one of six such vehicles delivered in mid-1973. (AS)

It wasn't just mainland operators who were quick to order the new Dominant, as 1974 saw the first of several delivered to Ulsterbus for use in their tours division. Leyland Leopard 1912 (HOI 1912) was a regular on the Western Highlands tour and is seen parked in Oban. (AS)

I love how far back those seats appear to go – makes you almost want to spend your 75p to go on the Four Forests Tour. Southdown's Leopard 1254 (CUF 254L), complete with sliding windows trying to entice tourists the traditional way with an (incorrectly) handwritten sandwich board propped against the side of the coach. (AS)

Taking a diagonal move from the south-east coast to the north-west coast, we find Ribble's Leopard 1032 (XTF 806L) parked outside Blackpool's Coliseum bus station. Originally new as express and tour coaches, by the time this photo was taken in 1982 many of the batch had been downgraded to local coach work – hence their NBC dual-purpose livery. (AS)

Seen travelling down Park Lane surrounded by some fantastic examples of 1970s automobilia is Chesterfield Transport's Dominant Express-bodied Leopard TNU 14M, one of only two Duple-bodied coaches purchased new by the undertaking. (AS)

When I consider the hours I spent around VCS in the 1980s and 1990s I can't recall having seen this particular livery layout (or for that matter that particular style of Hastings fleet name), although the south-east services did leave from further down the station from us lot going to the south-west, so perhaps it's not that surprising. The driver of former Maidstone & District PKM 114M receives his parking-up instructions prior to working the 037 back to Bexhill via Hastings. (AS)

With the statue of Churchill looking down in the background, it can only be Parliament Square where we see Windsorian of Windsor's VYM 507M, a Bedford YRT which had been new to National Travel (South East) in 1973. The coach was less than four years old when caught on camera, the lighter-weight coaches not tending to spend long with the NBC coaching units. (AS)

The passengers only had to travel one way; the drivers had to do both! London to Aberdeen on a grant-spec Ford R1014 must have been a delightful journey with that turbocharged lump screaming away at the front of the coach. New in 1973, Northern Scottish NT78 (PRS 720M) is seen trundling down Buckingham Palace Road ready for the long trip back to the granite city. (AS)

I've commented on it in previous books, but every picture I've included of Cardiff it's been raining, so let's just stay with the theme. To give Duple their due, they did do a comfy seat, and the rake on those in Western Welsh's UC474 (RBO 194M) looks like you'd soon fall asleep! The 10-metre Leopard PSU4/Dominant combination wasn't the most common, but the little coach remained in South Wales until 1988 before being acquired by Davies Bros of Pencader, who had it rebodied with a Willowbrook Warrior bus body. (AS)

Edinburgh is architecturally probably the most beautiful city in Scotland, and the lovely properties behind Waverley Bridge do nothing to detract from that. Lothian Region Transport (and Edinburgh Corporation before it) operated a fleet of coaches in this distinctive black and white livery, including 206 (NFS 206M), one of ten Dominant Express-bodied Bedford YRTs delivered in 1973 to Edinburgh Corporation. (AS)

Charterplan, Godfrey Abbott, Lancashire United Coaches, and Warburtons Travel, the four constituents of Greater Manchester PTE's coaching division, all carried a common livery style but with the stripes a different two-tone for each of the fleets. I always thought the two blues of Warburtons to be the most attractive, as seen on Leopard YNA 400M seen arriving at Wembley in 1973. (AS)

Staying in the north-west (although down in the south-east) we see a 12-metre-long Leopard PSU5 in the distinctive green and black of Robinsons of Great Harwood. 172 (VTB 972M) was the second of an identical pair (trust me when I say sister ship 171 is parked next to 172) delivered in 1973, and they are seen parked at the rear of the Claremont Hotel in Eastbourne. (AS)

Throughout the 70s and 80s, Grey-Green and its sister companies Worldwide, Orange and Dix standardised on the Duple Dominant and here is the very first one delivered. Bedford YMT VLB 669M was one of three similar vehicles delivered in 1974 and is seen in Eastbourne. (AS)

You always feel safe nestled between a pair of big Bristols, so no wonder the driver of Safeguard of Guildford's Leopard HPG 30N looks so happy. It later passed to another safe, that being Safeway of South Petherton. (AS)

To exemplify how versatile the Dominant was (and also show what I was wittering on about in on page 15) we see Charterplan's 92 (JND 992N), a thirty-seat Bristol LHS parked in United Counties' Luton depot. One of two delivered in June 1975, they were joined by a third the following year. Only twenty Dominant coach bodies were fitted to Bristol chassis, all of which were LHs. (AS)

I know it's from the same fleet, but Charterplan's Leopard 94 (JND 994N) is worthy of inclusion for several reasons, not least the two different style number 9s on its registration plate. It boasted luxuries we now take for granted, such as a toilet and, as can be seen by the subtle pod at the rear, air conditioning. Its side profile is also different due to it having flat glass glazing. (AS)

The rear axle track on Brenton's of Blackheath's 10-metre Leopard PSU4 GBB 997N looked so narrow I originally thought it was an older chassis rebodied, but no, it was new to Tyne & Wear PTE in 1975. With the air-con on full, it is seen arriving at Epsom on Derby Day. (AS)

Carrying almost a reverse livery to the above is Premier – Albanian of Watford's Bedford YRT HVD 585N. We take for granted now that filling stations are open round the clock and you have to serve yourself, but back in the 1970s it was clearly a novelty. Having to take oil home to regularly top up the engine, however, wasn't. (AS)

The front-mounted engine on Bedford's SB chassis range meant that the original Dominant body was fitted to this chassis until the end of Bedford production in 1988, ending the strong Bedford-Duple partnership which had been in place for over fifty years. Boon's of Boreham in Essex were the first operators of forty-one-seat Bedford SB5 HRT 530N, seen when new in 1975. It later passed to fellow Essex operator Amos of Belchamp St Paul before ending up as a traveller home. (AS)

Also seen when brand new is JGP 237N, a Bristol LHL new to Fred Wilde's Mitcham Belle fleet. One of three Dominants purchased new in 1975 (a pair of Bristols and a Seddon Pennine VI) fitted with extra marker lights along the roof and extra side indicators, it is seen in Princes Park coach park in Eastbourne. The Bristol chassis was always easy to identify as the narrow track of both axles made the body appear too wide for the chassis. (AS)

Now here is a first! The very first DAF chassis to be delivered to a British operator was JNK 554N, new to Robinson's of Appleby. It was the only original Dominant-bodied DAF to be delivered, and it was to be a further six years before any more DAFs were bodied by Duple. It is seen at Blackpool's Coliseum coach station on hire to National Travel (North-West) on one of those busy summer Saturdays I remember from childhood holidays. Note the body differences: lower side skirts, no ribbed trim under the windows and the windscreen mounted slightly lower than usual with the bottom edge not lining up with the bottom of the cab window. (AS)

Talking of Blackpool, one of the most unusual direct coach services that popped up after the deregulation of Great Britain's long-distance coach services was the City Flyer, operated by Burnley & Pendle, Leicester City Transport and Maidstone Borough Council. The service initially ran between Blackpool and Dover via Sheffield, Leicester and London, but over time contracted as operators withdrew from the consortium. Seen departing from Aldgate bus station with a healthy load is Burnley's Leopard 4 (YHG 4N). (AS)

Seen taking part in the 1975 Brighton Coach Rally is Bedford YRT HER 667N, the Cambridge United football team coach operated by Young's of Cambridge. Carrying the Cambridge team colours, unlike the lavishly equipped team coaches of today, apart from the back-to-back seats and tables, the one nod to luxury was the fitting of a small optic bar at the rear – Cambridge obviously had their priorities right! (AS)

Here it is: the original Duple Goldliner. I went into detail about the chassis in my Bedford book (shameless plug…), so here it's just about the body. As can be seen, Bedford YRT JKX 742N's body was higher than a standard Dominant but retained the standard front end so had an extended height destination box. After its demonstration days were over it passed to Tricentrol of Dunstable where its more powerful experimental turbocharged engine made it a favourite amongst the drivers. (AS)

HNU 118N was one of Nottingham's eighteen 'Lilac Leopards', purchased specifically to operate dedicated park and ride services under the ill-fated Zone & Collar initiative proposed by Nottinghamshire County Council in 1975. Designed to reduce car movement into the city centre, the short-lived scheme was abandoned in 1976 after a change of political control, and most of the Lilac Leopards went to Maidstone. (AS)

From little acorns, mighty oaks do grow. Volvo B58 LYS457P was one of a pair delivered new to Park's of Hamilton, allegedly from a cancelled order for Australia, their specification including sliding windows and seats trimmed in vinyl and leather. It was involved in quite a nasty accident early in its life but was rebuilt and returned to service. It later joined GT Travel of Perth where it became the first coach to carry their new trading name – Stagecoach. Wonder what happened to them after that?! (AS)

Out of the eleven 'NDF' AEC Reliances delivered to National Travel (South West), 155 remained on the books for several years after its counterparts had been withdrawn and passed into the Wessex fleet when NTSW was disbanded. It was repainted in a dark blue livery and operated the service between Bristol Parkway railway station and Bristol Airport. It is seen here in VCS waiting time before running back to 'Brizzle'. (AS)

Another major operator making the Dominant one of their staple purchases during the 70s and 80s was Wallace Arnold. Leopard NNW 106P is seen on an Eastbourne-based tour undertaking one of its day excursions on hire to Southdown. The licensing regulations in place at the time presumably meant Wallace Arnold didn't hold the required licence for that particular day's destination. (AS)

I'm not sure about the additional brightwork at the front of Bebb of Llantwit Fardre's 12-metre fifty-seven-seat AEC Reliance JWO 40P; it gives the impression of either being unfinished or removed due to damage. With one of the famous Twin Towers in the background, the location can only be the old Wembley Stadium. (AS)

Another football club executive ... this time Garelochhead Coaches' Ford MUS 102P which acted as Dumbarton FC's team coach. In this case, the 'executive' moniker referred to the coach having a couple of tables fitted towards the rear when taking The Sons (short for Sons of the Rock) to their away fixtures. (AS)

Formed in 1961, Luton-based Britannia Airways became the world's largest holiday airline before being rebranded as Thomsonfly in 2004. Being also based in Luton, Seamarks were ideally placed to undertake inter-airport transfers and had several coaches painted in full Britannia airways livery, one being Ford R1114 ONK 841P. (AS)

In order to serve the narrow roads and bridges across Dartmoor, Wallace Arnold's Devon fleet had four PSU4 Leopards fitted with special 7-foot 6-inch-wide bodies, their nearside windscreens narrower than the offside ones. NNW 98P is seen in Plymouth's Bretonside bus station, the Embankment in the nearside destination glass referring to Embankment Motor Co. of Plymouth, taken over by Wallace Arnold in 1974. (AS)

A new variant of the Dominant Express was developed in conjunction with City of Nottingham. Known as the Dominant E, it utilised a standard Dominant Express body shell, but with the majority of the stainless steel external trim deleted, top sliding windows fitted in lieu of forced air ventilation, no luggage racks and bus seats instead of coach seats. Twenty-six were built, two for Paton Bros of Renfrew, the rest, including 762 (MTV 762P), for Nottingham, all on Leopard chassis. (AS)

Yelloway only bought two Dominants and, as expected of this superb company, both were on AEC Reliance chassis. NNC 850P, seen here, was 11 metres long and NNC 855P was 12 metres long. Fitted with only forty-four seats, 850P is seen in Bristol Docks coach park on a South-West Clipper express service in 1979. 855P was scrapped in the early 1990s but 850P survives to this day, based at the Bury Transport Museum, and houses the Yelloway mobile museum created by the late, great 'Mr Yelloway', David Haddock. (AS)

The Royal Arsenal Co-operative Society (RACS) was a consumer co-operative based in south-east London, and took its name from the Royal Arsenal munitions works in Woolwich. To support its retail activities it had fingers in many pies, including a frozen food plant, an abattoir, a dairy and a fleet of coaches which ran under both the RACS and Duval & Sons names. One of the former was Leopard MHX 532P, one of five identical vehicles purchased new in 1975/6. (AS)

If you thought the Charterplan Bristol LHS seen earlier was short, then just take a look at this little beauty. One of three delivered in 1976 (the other two of which had bus seats in a coach shell), not only were they even shorter than a standard LHS due to the rear overhang being reduced, they were also only 7 feet 6 inches wide. All three had sliding windows, non-standard side trim and no forced air ventilation. 342 (PHG 242P) later passed to Jersey-based Pioneer where it must have been an ideal vehicle for operating on the island. (AS)

Carrying National Travel (West) fleet names, I think this photo was taken when control of that part of the NBC empire had passed to Ribble as I'm sure that when NTW was a separate entity, their fleet numbers were prefixed with an 'N' and were four-figure numbers (or maybe I just need to get out more…). Seen at speed on the M1 near Hemel Hempstead is 15 (URN 215R) which was new to National Travel (North-West) in 1976. It was part of a batch originally ordered with Alexander M-type bodies, but switched to Duple before building began. (AS)

Staying in the north-west we see our first photo of probably the largest coach operator in the area. Having been loyal Plaxton customers for many years, Wigan-based Smiths Happiway-Spencers switched allegiance to Duple in 1976, and between then and 1986 received over 250 examples. AEC Reliance 35 (ODJ 53R) carries the registration plate originally fitted to the prototype Dominant II REK 929R when it was displayed at the 1977 Commercial Motor Show. (AS)

Another major Shropshire operator no longer with us is Vagg of Knockin Heath, formed as Vagg Motors in the 1920s as a partnership between Steve and John Vagg. Fifty years of family ownership came to an end in 1974 when the partnership sold out to the T.E. Jones Group, who kept the Vagg's name (although changed to Vaggs Coaches) until the early 1980s when the group went into receivership and Vaggs was no more. Delivered after the takeover and seen in Weston-super-Mare was Express-bodied Ford R1114 OUJ 185R. (AS)

As mentioned earlier, with the introduction of the Dominant II the original Dominant received a facelift and became known as the Dominant I. Bedford YMT OYV703R was new to World Wide Travel of London in September 1976, World Wide at the time being a subsidiary of Grey-Green's owners the Ewer Group, having been purchased from American Express to give the group a presence in the incoming tourist market. (AS)

Urban myth or fact? No one will really know if Ian Fleming picked the code name for James Bond based on the route number of the coach service from London to Dover, but he did once live in Ebury Street (right behind VCS) before moving to Kent, so who knows? It is, however, still today the number of the National Express service between the capital and Kent. 6540 FN was originally fitted to a Park Royal-bodied AEC Reliance, later rebodied with a Plaxton Panorama Elite, but by the 1990s had been assigned to Leopard 8794, formerly PJG 794S. (AS)

For over a hundred years, Clynnog & Trefor have been providing transportation to the good people of north-east Wales, today operating a fleet of high-end luxury coaches. Back in the mid-1980s, local services on the Bws Gwynedd network were in the hands of former Potteries Leopard PEH 49R, seen loading in Caernarfon's old bus station. (AS)

Eastern Counties Leopard LL756 (SPW 102R) was one of four similar vehicles delivered in May 1977 in National white but equipped for one-man operation (as it was known back then) from new. In 1981, the quartet received this simple red and white livery for use on the joint ECOC/London Country (Green Line) services 797/8 between VCS and Cambridge, the coach having just arrived in the capital, the manual Setright ticket machine clearly visible. (AS)

An even more dedicated livery is carried by Brighton & Hove's Leopard 189 (RYJ 889R), that for the Sealine 773 service between Brighton and Guildford. New to Southdown, it was originally fitted with two top sliding windows on each side, but as can be seen the sliders were replaced by fixed glass panels, which begs the question why not just replace the whole side window? (AS)

NBC subsidiaries were expected to toe the party line and paint buses either leaf green or poppy red; however, some decided to buck the trend, including Jones of Aberbeeg, a forty-vehicle-strong South Wales independent sold to the NBC in April 1969. Until 1981, despite being under the control of Red & White, buses in the Jones fleet were painted blue. Coaches, however, did conform (well, apart from the blue fleet name) as can be seen by Leopard UC2.77 (PKG 724R) making a rather spirited entrance into Parliament Square. (AS)

Glenton Tours of London were renowned for their centre entrance touring coaches. The seats (usually only thirty-four or thirty-eight to a coach) were staggered so all passengers had an uninterrupted view to the side. They standardised on Plaxton bodies, but in 1977 took delivery of three Dominant I-bodied Volvo B58s. No more Duples were ordered, and all three were later rebodied by Plaxton. Seen on Belgrave Road in Pimlico is the middle of the three, PYT 153R. (AS)

Whilst it is acknowledged that the majority of Dominant Is were delivered to NBC subsidiaries, new ones did find their way into independent hands. Leopard ONL 772R was new to Tyne Valley of Acomb in 1977 and is seen at Wembley carrying several members of the AS fan club. (AS)

Fountain Coaches, based in Cowes on the Isle of Wight, was formed after the First World War and remained independent until 1967 when acquired by the state-owned THC subsidiary Shamrock & Rambler. In 1969, management of Fountain transferred to Southern Vectis, who continued to use the name as part of their coaching operations. Bedford YMT 126 (TDL 126S) is seen parked in Ventnor garage in 1989, looking immaculate for an eleven-year-old coach. (AS)

When G.K. Kinch of Mountsorrel won the contract to provide vehicles for Leicestershire's Access bus services, they converted a couple of Leopards including ex-Southdown VCD 294S to allow wheelchair access at the rear. At this time, Kinch had built a reputation as a very high-end coach operator, well known for running full-size coaches with only around thirty seats in them, but they were usually used for transporting footballers rather than OAPs! (AS)

I'm surprised the nearside front wheel isn't rubbing on the arches with the amount of lean on City of Oxford's ex-Potteries Leopard 50 (URF 50S). Lettered up for the 190 Oxford–London service, I didn't notice until researching for this book that the nearside of coaches in this livery had Oxford–London and the offside had London–Oxford. (AS)

What a variety of NBC names in one location: one South Midland, two Wessex and, the focus of the picture, one Hampshire Coach, whose Leopard 3033 (WFH 165S) is seen at Oxford's Gloucester Green bus station in 1984. New to National Travel (South West), it still retained the alternate red and blue seats synonymous with NBC coaches from the mid-1970s. (AS)

The Invictaway brand was introduced in the early 1980s for Maidstone & District's services from the Medway Towns into London, as well as the 900 service to Gatwick Airport. The distinctive black livery included the white horse of Kent as a visual link to the county the services were serving. Leopard 2152 (BKJ 152T) is seen on layover at Gatwick coach park having operated the 900. (AS)

During busy periods, coaches more suitable to local work would be pressed into use on long-distance express services. Fife Scottish FPE133 (GSG 133T), a 1978 Leopard, makes a welcome break from the usual National white when seen at VCS in 1981 after having duplicated an Anglo-Scottish service. Immaculately presented, with wheel trims front and rear, it would usually be used on tours and inter-urban work out of St Andrew's depot (AS)

Aberconwy Borough Council Bedford VAS5 BUR 430T seen awaiting custom for a circular tour of Llandudno and the Great Orme. This coach was new to Glynglen of West Drayton in 1978 and joined the tiny Aberconwy fleet in 1985. (AS)

Tyne & Wear PTE took over the long-established fleets of Armstrong's of Westerhope and Galley's of Newcastle and renamed the combined fleets as Armstrong-Galley. 78 (CBB 478V), a 1979 Leopard, is seen at King's Cross coach station in London, now the site of the British Library. (AS)

With the lovely Park Hill estate in the background (given Grade II* listed status in 1998), we see South Yorkshire PTE's Leopard 19 (JKW 219W) waiting time in Sheffield Pond Street bus station. A very late model Dominant I, the deep ribbed chrome strip under the windows (sources advise) was removed due to it causing corrosion damage. (AS)

Dominant II

For the 1975 season, Plaxton, Duple's main rival, introduced a completely new design known as the Supreme, and, not wanting to be left behind, Duple decided to revamp the Dominant. They did so by employing the services of famed Italian designer Giovanni Michelotti, resulting in the Dominant II, a design owing much to the original Dominant, retaining the deep side windows and ribbed steel trim but with completely redesigned front and back ends. At the front, a much deeper windscreen was used which lined up with the driver's side window, which in turn met up with the lower edge of the side trim. So deep was the windscreen that the whole of the driving binnacle could be seen from the front of the coach. Gone were the circular headlights, replaced by two flush-fitting rectangular units either side of a small rectangular grille. At the rear, the window became a shallow one-piece flat glass affair, and the light units were now horizontal rather than vertical, although vertical assemblies could be specified as a special order. The Dominant II was fitted to the majority of chassis that its predecessor was built on, apart from the Ford R-Series with non-tilted engine or the forward-engined Bedford SB and VAS, as their engine location combined with the smaller grille on the Dominant II required them to be fitted with the original Dominant, which now became known as the Dominant I and received a revamped front end. As with the Dominant, the Dominant II could be ordered to grant specification and the split full-length glass doors were carried over to the new design.

Seen in the demonstration park at the 1976 Earl's Court Motor Show is one of the pre-production Dominant II bodies. Fitted to a Bedford YMT chassis, note the different centre grille panel, smaller headlights and lower door window and how the chrome strip under the side windows curves up at the front, unlike on production models where it carried on into the doorframe. The coach subsequently passed to Price of Halesowen and was registered WUY 925R. (AS)

Despite the growing popularity of the chassis, the first year of Dominant II production saw only two R-registered Volvo B58s delivered. Battersby Silver Grey of Morecambe took one of them (as well as an identical vehicle on an S plate later in the year), ACK 7R. (AS)

Above and below: OOO Olau! National Travel (London) differed from the rest of the National Travel fleets in that rather than provide dedicated coaches for National Express services, they worked more on incoming tourist work, hence the slip board brackets by the fleet name. The unusual windscreen-washer system fitted to AEC Reliance OYU 571R had disappeared by the time I was to be found cleaning the coach when it moved to (what was then) my local operator, Roselyn of Cornwall, when less than six years old. (AS/HB collection)

I'd love to know how much rail was involved in Chesterfield Transport's tour programme to justify having it on the destination blind. Express-bodied Leopard OWJ 16R was sold when less than three years old, and there is the possibility the coach may have had its front end rebuilt due to accident damage as photographs of it in its subsequent life show not only a different front dome but also a one-piece coach door. (AS)

Grey-Green were quick off the mark to order the Dominant II, taking a batch of thirty in 1977, all but two of which were Bedford YMTs, including RYL 721R in 1979. It was one of three coaches selected to receive potential new liveries, thankfully not the one chosen when the experiment ended. (AS)

What a cracking picture! This epitomises everything I remember about 1970s coaches: those lovely AEC front wheels and the Dominant body lying low on the chassis. Powering its way round Broad Quay in Bristol, the passengers aboard Smiths Happiway-Spencers' Reliance WED 989S seem really happy about going on tour to Minehead… (AS)

At first glance this appears to be a standard NBC Dominant; it's only when you look at the small one-piece destination blind you realise it's not. Bedford YMT SVJ 300S was new to Yeoman's of Hereford and was acquired by Midland Red (West) when they purchased Yeoman's Hereford–London service to eliminate competition with the National Express service. It is rather ironic that nowadays the National Express service from Hereford to London is operated by Yeoman's. (AS)

Until closure in 1988, Bexleyheath Transport, one of several companies associated with the Margo family, would take delivery of up to ten new coaches every year – predominantly Bedfords fitted with either Plaxton or Duple bodies. The 1978 order contained two Dominant II-bodied Bedford YLQs, including TPJ 284S. (AS)

Wallace Arnold had so many Dominants it was difficult to decide which ones to include, so I plumped for Leopard WUG 150S as it's ever so slightly different. Allocated as the designated team coach for Leeds United Football Club, the eagle eyed will notice that as well as the pod on the roof for TV reception, it also has flat glass rather than curved, which is usually an indication that the windows were double glazed – in this case experimental toughened glass. It is seen here at Wembley carrying members of Leeds' other shaped ball team. (AS)

Orange Luxury Coaches of Brixton was acquired by the Ewer Group in 1953, together with the ornately fronted coach station in Effra Road, Brixton (built in 1927 and was the first motor coach station in London). Remaining as a separate subsidiary of Grey-Green until wound up in December 1975, coaches continued to wear the Orange livery, name and more importantly the queen's arms, as Orange was the supplier of coaches to the royal household. Bedford YMT TYE 702S is seen in Parliament Square when new in 1978. (AS)

Yes, it is a Dommy II. City of Oxford's Leopard 13 (RFC 13T) was one of a pair whose front ends were rebuilt with the style of front fitted to the Dominant III and IV usually for the SBG. It later had an even more radical rebuild when its Dominant body was replaced with a Willowbrook Warrior bus body. It is seen in Oxford Gloucester Green coach station in 1983. (AS)

Originally based in the small Devon village of Yelverton, F.G. Trathen and Sons went on to become one of the big players in the 1980s coaching scene, not only in (initially) competing with National Express when they started the 'Rapide' service between the west of England and London, but also operating the first Neoplan Skyliner in the UK. They were also early users of the Volvo B58 and their 1979 order of twenty-one saw Caetano, Van Hool and Irizar bodies enter the fleet. There were however seven Dominant IIs in the order including SDR 447T, seen arriving at Wembley. (AS)

When Britain's coach services were deregulated in October 1980, as well as operators like Trathens competing over single routes, a consortium of leading independent operators formed British Coachways to compete with National Express and the SBG at a network level. Most vehicles retained their owners' livery, but a small number received British Coachways livery including Wallace Arnold's Leopard CED 203T (which unusually for WA was purchased second-hand, from Shadwell of Warrington), seen in King's Cross coach station, London, in 1981. (AS)

Earlier, we saw a Grey-Green coach in a rather garish experimental livery, which thankfully the company decided against. They did however, plump for the style seen in the picture above, which probably looks familiar as it's the same as the one in the previous picture! When Grey-Green withdrew from British Coachways they decided they actually quite liked the livery so adopted and adapted it to suit their own fleet colours. (AS)

NBC subsidiary London Country was desperate to halt the decline in patronage on its Green Line network, so in 1977 commenced a fleet modernisation plan with the lease from Anston-based Kirkby Central of 150 AEC Reliances. They were delivered over a three-year period and consisted of sixty Plaxton (RS class) and ninety Duple (RB class). Seen parked on London's Eccleston Bridge in the company of three RSs is RB80 (YPL 80T).

Acting as a combined Leyland demonstrator and transport for the Leyland Motors Band when new, Leopard MCK 301T had a short and rather sad life. Not long after being sold to Rennies of Dunfermline, it was used on a private hire to Blackpool where it was stolen from the coach park and driven onto the beach. It became so bogged down it was unable to be rescued before being destroyed by the tide. It is seen in happier times undertaking its original role at Brighton. (AS)

At first glance it could be the same coach; however, this is CTM 407T, one of six Dominant-bodied Leopards purchased by Guards of London in 1979. Guards had only been formed in 1970 (by an ex-Grenadier Guardsman) but still managed to purchase fifty new coaches in a decade. (AS)

Delivered new to National Travel (South West's) Wessex division as a standard fifty-three seater in 1978, Leopard 187 (AFH 187T) was soon upgraded to executive specification complete with TV and bar and was named Wessexecutive II (the original Wessexecutive being Plaxton Supreme-bodied Bedford YMT MOU 505R). As well as being the Bristol Rovers team coach, it was also the official team coach for visiting international cricket teams, and is seen parked in VCS whilst carrying the Pakistan team in 1981. Like NDF 155P seen earlier, it too ended its days with Wessex on the dedicated service to Bristol Airport.

Sister ship 190 (AFH 190T) was one of several NBC coaches to receive this blue and white livery for undertaking work on behalf of P&O. East Kent, Maidstone & District, National Travel (London), Hants & Dorset, and Southdown also had vehicles in the livery for undertaking P&O Landtours whilst 190 was the dedicated vehicle for the P&O Ferries service from Cheltenham to Paris. (AS)

In 1980, Southend Transport and Reading Transport commenced operating the X1, a joint service between their respective towns via Heathrow Airport and London. Two years later the partnership was disbanded, both operators still running an X1 of their own with Southend's now terminating at Heathrow. In May 1982, passenger loadings saw several short- and long-term coach hires taking place as well as the introduction of a peak hours only X21 from Shoeburyness to Green Park, and seen operating it is the first coach to be hired, Colchester's Leopard DHK 102T. (AS)

Ahead of the privatisation of the NBC in 1986, several of the larger subsidiaries were split into smaller operating units to make their sale more manageable, Ribble being one of them. The company's depots across Merseyside and Manchester were transferred to a new company which revived an old name – North Western. Lightly loaded Leopard 703 (BNB 239T), new to National Travel (West), swings into Preston bus station en route to Blackpool in 1987. (AS)

Eastern Counties was another of the NBC subsidiaries to be split up, with the depots in Cambridgeshire and parts of Suffolk passing to a new company known as Cambus, who adopted this attractive pale blue livery. Seen arriving at Peterborough is Leopard 409 (XYK 767T) which had been new to Grey-Green, one of six coaches passing to Cambus in March 1985 after Grey-Green withdrew from the East Anglian express joint service with NBC. I'm not sure what the occasion was, but there seems to be quite a lot of camera-based enthusiast activity taking place – perhaps they'd heard that AS was there and wanted some tips. (AS)

The Tricentrol empire was a substantial business, with one of its many arms being Tricentrol Chassis Developments who took the standard 11-metre-long Bedford YMT chassis and extended it to 12 metres, thus making the first Bedford chassis of this length and predating the manufacturer's own chassis of that length by some eight years. Only about twenty conversions were done – the extra length required mesh luggage racks to be fitted to keep the weight down. Young's of Rampton's WER 477T was one of these, the mesh racks visible above the driver's head. (AS)

Having bought their first Volvos only the previous year, Wallace Arnold went for the marque with some gusto in 1979, purchasing fifteen, just under half of that year's new vehicle order. The writing was on the wall for Leyland and Ford, WA's previous chassis suppliers, and before long the big Swede was to become the company's chassis of choice. Seen passing St George's House (later to become the Nestle Tower) on Park Lane in Croydon (Wallace Arnold had a small depot there after acquiring the tour licences of Homeland Tours in 1948) is EWW 227T. (AS)

As well as now being in a different location, the Hanley bus station of today has nowhere near the variety of colours we can see here. Mixing with the poppy red and multicoloured all-over advert, Bristol VRs of local NBC subsidiary Potteries, we also have the red and white of Stonier of Goldenhill's ex-Bournemouth Weymann-bodied Leyland Atlantean. The focal point of the picture, however, is Northern Scottish Leopard NPE 98 (HSA 98V) heading for Aberdeen with a healthy load in 1982. (AS)

As might be expected of a Lancastrian municipality, Fylde Borough Transport (and its predecessor Lytham St Anne's Corporation) was a staunch Leyland operator; however, it broke with tradition in 1980 by purchasing a solitary Volvo B58, 28 (XRN 28V). The motor survived long enough to pass to Blackpool Transport when Fylde was acquired in 1994 and finished its days in North Wales. (AS)

I spent a good half-hour searching for the exact location where AS took this picture of Lancaster City Council's Dominant Express-bodied Leopard 12 (URN 12V), and using a combination of Google, Flickr and Old Maps Online I finally worked out it was turning off North Road into Damside Street bus station. My smugness disappeared when one of my colleagues walked past, looked over my shoulder and casually commented, 'Ahh, that looks like Damside Street in Lancaster…' (AS)

Staying in Lancashire, we see a coach that did just that! New as Ribble's 1141 in 1980, WCK 141V was sold 'just down the road' to Mercers of Longridge in Preston and is seen in its hometown's bus station. Despite looking rather down at heel (and down at the back end), it did go on to finally leave the red rose county when it passed to Irvine's of Law. (AS)

Just because you want a smaller vehicle, you don't have to settle for a minibus… and how lovely does Grey-Green's Bedford CYH 797V look? As well as being one of several Bedford YLQs shortened to 8-metres by Tricentrol, it was also a star of stage and screen, featuring in a 1981 episode of *Grange Hill* when Tucker Jenkins and his cronies went on an ill-fated trip to France. (AS)

Following deregulation in 1986, West Yorkshire PTE rebranded itself as Yorkshire Rider and at the same time gave Metro Coach, its coaching unit, a revamp, this becoming Gold Rider. As well as undertaking the company's longer-distance express services, Gold Rider also operated private hires. Former Fox of Hayes Leopard 1539 (NLP 172V), complete with the black-painted window surrounds that were *en vogue* at the time, is seen doing just that as it powers down Cumberland Gate in London. (AS)

I put this in as another of those non-standard NBC Dominants and by pure coincidence it too is also ex-Fox of Hayes. Whilst to the casual observer Leopard 1305 (LLT 346V) might look like a standard NBC Dominant, the additional side trim, lack of Bristol dome, destination equipment and of course the seats trimmed in a decidedly non-NBC moquette make it stand out as something not quite the norm. Seen in VCS operating Eastern National's standard National Express service, the 084 to Walton-on-the-Naze. (AS)

I mentioned earlier the large AEC Reliance order for Green Line, which was planned to be thirty coaches a year over a five-year period from 1977. However, increased patronage and the announcement that the Reliance was to be discontinued saw the final sixty delivered in 1979. A year later, five were painted in a special livery to celebrate fifty years of Green Line, one being RB135 (EPM 135V, seen in St Peter's Street, St Albans). The end of the Reliance meant a replacement had to be found, and in order to find one, two Volvo B58s and two Leopards, all with Dominant bodies, were put head-to-head on the northern orbital route 734. Whilst the quieter Volvos were more passenger friendly, drivers liked the Leopard's big engine and engineers found the working bits easier to get to, so the Leopard won. Smoking Volvo DV2 (GPH 2V) is seen turning off Buckingham Palace Road onto Eccleston Bridge. (AS)

An early acquisition by the fledgling Stagecoach was Volvo B58 FVO 661V, new to Kettlewell's of Retford in 1979. Back in the days when destination gear consisted of plastic signs in the window, the coach is seen whilst operating the Pitlochry to Perth service. (RS)

Erewash Valley Services was formed in 1988 when Stevensons of Spath sold their Ilkeston area operations to Nottingham City Transport. New to Stevensons in 1980 as LFA872V, Leopard AEH 607A is seen entering the coach station at London Heathrow in 1989. I remember that Rover Sterling very well – a lovely looking car that got more weatherbeaten the longer it was up there. (AS)

I can't believe the last time I drove a Leopard was over thirty years ago, but it was, and it was the sister to the coach shown here – 64 (GRF 264V). Potteries made good use of their operating initials of PMT when designing the logo for their ParaMounT Leisure business, which survived well into privatisation before being sold to Leon's of Stafford in 1993. It is funny to think that fifteen years after driving that ex-PMT Leopard I would be their Operations Manager. (AS)

When East Kent was sold to its management in 1987, coaches retained a pseudo-NBC 'Venetian blind livery' but in East Kent's new cherry red and cream colours, as seen on Leopard 8815 (XJG 814V). As can be seen by the frontage of Dover depot, the old East Kent Road Car Company name was quickly being replaced with the new red and white EK logo. (AS)

Prior to Fox of Hayes ceasing operations in 1983, their Dominant-bodied Leopards were taken back into stock by Arlington, the Potters Bar-based dealers who supplied them in the first place. The majority were sold to NBC subsidiaries, MNK 427V being one of four acquired by Alder Valley. As can be seen, it later passed to Osborne's of Tollesbury, where it was caught in Colchester bus station in company of another NK-registered coach, A382 NNK, Arlington's Leyland Royal Tiger demonstrator. (AS)

Northwest Coachlines of Kirkham operated a daily service linking Douglas on the Isle of Man to London King's Cross coach using the Manxline ferry operating into the port of Heysham. Kicking up a cloud of dust as it races away from King's Cross is Volvo B58 GRN 896W, one of a quartet of identical vehicles bought new in 1981. (AS)

Maidstone Boro'line's Bedford YMT SGS 505W was one of nineteen consecutively registered coaches delivered through dealer Ensign of Greys. The batch included Bedfords and Leylands (two different models of each), plus Volvo and AEC chassis, and Duple, Plaxton and Van Hool bodies. It was the first coach delivered new to Stephenson of Hullbridge, now known as Stephensons of Essex with a fleet of over 100 vehicles, Boro'line going the other way, having completely disappeared. (AS)

Another operator sadly no longer with us is Davies of Pencader, for many years the largest family-owned passenger vehicle operator in Wales. Having bought their first bus in 1925, the company served the good people of Carmarthenshire until 1999 when financial difficulties saw the company enter receivership. In happier times, Leopard 124 (YBX 917V) waits in Carmarthen bus station with a tantalising list of destinations, including four days in London with a show for £39. (RS)

If you're thinking that the livery on Thamesdown's GHR 301W looks similar to that on the Tyne Valley of Acomb coach we saw earlier, then you'd be correct. In 1980, Tyne Valley ordered four Dominant-bodied Leopards but cancelled two of them after they were painted, so Thamesdown took the pair. Both retained the livery until repainted in 1984 but carried the strange large font registration plates until sold. (AS)

Well, there's a first: Cardiff with the sun out (if you've bought my other books, you'll know what I'm on about). With the impressive Wales Empire Pool (built as the showpiece building for the 6th British Empire and Commonwealth Games hosted by the city in 1958), Cardiff's Leopard GTG 633W turns into Wood Street to access the bus station. AS is getting some quizzical looks from the passengers, probably amazed at seeing one of those new-fangled picture-taking machines. (AS)

Based in Bishopbriggs, Strathclyde, Kelvin Scottish was the largest of the four new companies created in 1985 by the SBG in readiness for deregulation (the name coming from the River Kelvin, a tributary of the River Clyde) and inherited nearly 400 vehicles from the Midland and Central Scottish fleets. From the former came Leopard 3061 (RWS 394W), seen in Blackpool with a coachful of excited holidaymakers. (AS)

Despite its Leopard chassis being built in 1979, Baildon Motors of Guisley didn't take delivery of VRY 610X until 1982. It is seen when almost fresh out of the box in Selby bus station. It later passed to the much-missed Bevan Brothers Soudley Valley Motors, who unsurprisingly did very little in terms of repaint as the two liveries were almost identical. (RS)

Dominant III and IV

For the 1981 season, the Dominant II was superseded by the Dominant III and IV. Both models shared the same front and rear ends, basically similar to the Dominant II save for the bumpers which were replaced by a beading inlaid rubber strip and the rear light clusters which, although still mounted horizontally, were arranged over two rows of lights which protruded out slightly between the two rows, this protrusion continuing along the bottom of the boot between the two light clusters. It was along the side of the body where the biggest change could be found: gone was the ribbed steel moulding, which led to a much crisper side profile. The Dominant IVs side profile was a subtle change, with the windows (which could be curved or flat glass) being slightly shallower than the Dominant II. However, the most radical feature of the two new models were the side windows of the Dominant III, which were shallow trapezoidal offerings similar to those found on the Alexander M-type body first introduced more than a decade earlier. Designed to look sleek and with more than a nod towards America's iconic Greyhound coaches, the wider-than-normal slanted window pillars meant that passengers sitting alongside a pillar had an interrupted view from the window. This contributed to the Dominant III being the least successful version of the Dominant range, with the largest orders going to the SBG for overnight Anglo-Scottish express services. For the first time (apart from a solitary example bodied in 1975), the mid-engined DAF MB range became available to be fitted with the Dominant IV. As with the previous incarnations of the Dominant, Duple were willing to 'mix and match', and as well as building a Dominant IV for Bostock's of Congleton, which had Dominant II windows for half its length, there were around a dozen Dominant IVs fitted with either one or two deeper windows towards the front and, as the windscreen on the Dominant I was cheaper than that on its successors, the NBC-specified Dominant IVs with Dominant I front and back ends.

I know it's a Dominant II, but I wanted it on the same page as the photo below, and the reduced brightwork does make it look like a Dominant IV. The first Leyland Tiger in the book, BHK 209X was delivered to Southend in 1982. Unusually for a coach built as recently as 1982, it's fitted with top sliding windows but no forced air ventilation, and was caught departing the Minories bus station in Aldgate en route for home. (AS)

One of a pair of Dominant III-bodied Leopards delivered to Excelsior of Dinnington in 1981, by 1984 KWG 130W had joined the Southend Transport fleet as No. 220. It is seen departing the Minories bus station with a right old lean on… (AS)

Sister KWG 121W moved leftwards when disposed of by Excelsior to join the Staffordshire fleet of Turner's of Brown Edge, a well-respected operator who over the years purchased a dozen new double-deckers to operate their regular service into Hanley. Turner's coaches wore green and ivory, whereas the buses were painted Tudor maroon and cream – allegedly easier to keep clean. (MH)

In 1987, the Turner's business was purchased by the newly privatised PMT and KWG 131W ended up on a regular service nearly back to its original home. I can only assume that at the time PMT didn't have a signwriter but did have a big roll of red tape lying around. Notice that despite passing through the hands of a rather conservative family operator, it's still carrying the big roof-mounted air horns it had fitted from new. (AS)

Back when VCS was almost exclusively used by the NBC, the only independents you'd typically see would be undertaking National Express duplicates. However, as the 453 service from Milton Keynes to London was operated by both Tricentrol and United Counties, Tricentrol used VCS by default. Seen arriving in the departure side of the station is brand-new Bedford YNT UMJ 420W, one of a batch of eleven Duple-bodied Bedfords purchased for Tricentrol and its subsidiaries in 1981. (AS)

Not quite what it seems, although the original Leopard badge on the grille is a bit of a clue. Barry Cooper of Warrington had a bit of a thing about rebodying older chassis, and Leopard OJP 908W was one of their many projects. Originally Plaxton Panorama-bodied WHA 252H, new to Midland Red in 1970, the chassis and that of sister WHA 229H were rebodied with Dominant IIIs. They were modified so much that new registrations were issued, however WHA 229H was kept back until August 1981 so it received an X suffix plate. (AS)

I was trying to work out what looked different about Whittle of Highley's Tricentrol converted 12-metre Bedford YNT KUX 234W, then realised it's the heavy-duty front bumper which several of Whittle's Dominant III and IVs carried. Goldhawk was the brand used for Whittle's services from various West Midlands locations to London King's Cross, which commenced in 1980. By 1981, Whittle's were operating the Goldhawk services in conjunction with National Express – hence the coach turning into VCS. (AS)

If I had to pick a favourite Duple body it would have to be one of these: a Dominant III fitted with the shallow Dominant I windscreen to accommodate a destination box above – a frontal style designed at the behest of the SBG. Seen in the company of one of the vehicles it was designed to emulate, the Alexander M type, is Eastern Scottish Tiger XH549 (BSG 549W). Eastern Scottish were the first operator to order the Tiger, and BSG 544W, the first of the batch, was one of the vehicles used for the model's lavish launch in Morocco. (AS)

We've seen the first coach to carry the Stagecoach name, so how about the first new coach bought? Seen on layover at King's Cross is Volvo B58 FES 831W, new to the company in 1981 and fitted with a toilet, which must have been a welcome luxury on those long Anglo-Scottish journeys. Later in its life it was rebuilt, losing its trapezoid windows in favour of conventional ones and being fitted with bus seats. Such a significant vehicle has now become one of the Stagecoach Group's preserved vehicles. (AS)

An operator I used to see regularly on visits to Blackpool was Bissett of Ryton-Upon-Tyne, who traded as Primrose. They operated a daily return service from Newcastle to Blackpool via Kirkby Stephen with the drop off/pick up at Turner's Rigby Road coach park, adjacent to Blackpool FC's Bloomfield Road ground, just visible in the background behind Tiger MTN 874X. (RS)

The SBG-style front wasn't exclusively fitted to motors from north of the border, and in 1982 Beeston's of Hadleigh had eight late model Leopards so fitted, with one being used as part of Duple's advertising campaign in Coachmart (remember that?). Two carried Beeston's name, including WGV 860X seen here, the others those of Beeston's constituent companies, Mulley's Motorways, Comb's and Corona. (AS)

Skill's of Nottingham purchased three Dominant IIIs with the SBG-style front including 21 (PVO 21X), a Volvo B58. Whether the Dominant III's styling was found to be unsuitable for the type of work Skill's had intended for them, who knows, but 21 and its siblings had very short lives with Skill's, being sold when scarcely a year old. (RS)

At first glance I thought RS had put a copyright banner across the picture, then realised it was the coach's livery! Bodies fitted to Ford chassis often seemed to ride 'high' and when combined with the narrow rear axle track gave the impression of being top heavy, as evidenced by H&M of Chasetown's Express-bodied R1114 YFD 198X. New to the company in 1982, it received a makeover which included this rather insipid livery and the grafting on of a Plaxton Paramount front panel and single headlights. Note it also has the later style of express doors, which were not fully glass. (RS)

I'm sure I remember this being on the cover of either *Buses* or *Buses Extra* when new, although it was over forty years ago. Gypsy Queen of Langley Park's Dominant III Express-bodied RJR 247Y was quite an unusual vehicle, being fitted to a Bedford YMT for a start. As it was the regular vehicle on the company's service to Durham, the destination display was painted on; it had a 'pay as you enter' sign fixed to the front and was fitted with bus seats. It must have been such a treat after climbing up those three or four high steps to then find that you couldn't even see out of the window! (RS)

Whilst its ZF 6-speed manual gearbox might have been perfect for trainees to get that all-important 'stick box' licence, I'm pretty sure that the high windows on Leopard PSC 621Y's body did nothing for their confidence when pulling out of junctions. Delivered new to (but finance, meaning it was possibly never operated by) Jack's of Cowdenbeath, it is seen here with Transtech Training Services, a division of Manchester College of Arts and Technology. (RS)

To finish off this short chapter, a Dominant III – or rather it was. By 1988, several of the SBG Dominant IIIs had been rebuilt with conventional side windows, some fitted with Dominant IV-sized windows, others with slightly deeper glass. Western's NCS 121W shows the unusual finish to the rear due to the original Dominant III windows not going right up to the back of the coach. (AS)

The first operator to put a Tiger on the road was Bostock's of Congleton with BCA 126W on 1 April 1981. The body was unusual, being one of the small number built with Dominant II windows at the front and Dominant IV at the rear, in this case all being double glazed. Leyland used the coach as a test bed during 1982, fitting the prototype 245bhp engine into it. Much to Peter Bostock's dismay, when Leyland finished with it they dropped the original 218bhp lump back! (MH)

As mentioned earlier, Green Line plumped for the Leopard as the replacement for the AEC Reliance. In 1981 they entered into a similar leasing arrangement with Kirkby, taking thirty, split between Plaxton and Duple. DL4 (MPL 124W) was one of a pair painted in this dedicated livery for the Fightline 767 between VCS and Heathrow. All were withdrawn in January 1986. (AS)

The KUX ***W batch of coaches delivered to Whittle's in 1980/1 contained five 12-metre-long PSU5 Leopards, including 46 (KUX 246W), all but two of which carried this heavy-duty bumper which made the coaches seem somehow more 'workmanlike'. None other than Mr Ron Whittle himself advised me that the bumpers were fitted to help minimise front end damage from 'comings together' on the narrow rural lanes the company operated over. Just visible on the left in this view of VCS is WFJ 930X, the third Neoplan Skyliner to enter traffic with Trathens. (AS)

A manual-box Leopard – lovely. Shortly after the end of the First World War, Alfred Smith bought an ex-army lorry. His mother-in-law suggested fitting it with a charabanc body, and from these humble beginnings Smith's Luxury Coaches of Reading grew to be one of southern England's largest coach companies. After Mr Smith's death, the company was sold to Windsorian. The vehicles retained their Smith's name but were repainted in Windsorian livery, as seen on KGM 329W. (AS)

Only ten DAFs received Dominant bodies. We saw the first way back in the early part of the book (p. 20), and this is the next one – six years later! JCF 640W was delivered to DAF as a demonstrator, and it retained this livery when passing to Wilfreda Beehive of Adwick le Street. Whilst working as a demonstrator it was used by Park's of Hamilton on the British Coachways service from Glasgow to London, its colours almost a perfect match for those used by the consortium. (MH)

I mentioned earlier that when Grey-Green withdrew from British Coachways they adopted the livery as their own. We can see that to good effect here on Leopard JYH 829W, one of a pair with SBG-style fronts purchased in 1980. (AS)

Remember what I said earlier about Ford chassis always looking too small for their bodies? Well, here is a good example: its Dominant IV Express body is riding high and the narrow rear axle is well inside the body. When Midland Fox took over N&S of Market Harborough, they modified N&S's livery into the semi-NBC Venetian blind livery seen on Ford R1114 7011 (NDW 39X), which had been new to Bebb of Llantwit Fardre. (AS)

There's something about that SBG-style front that makes the Dominant IV look so purposeful, especially when combined with a set of Leyland nut guard rings. Ebdon's of Sidcup's Tiger XGS 769X originally entered service in July 1981 registered UUR 348W, but somehow the company managed to get it re-registered in August 1981 to carry the X plate seen here. It later became one of the coaches that passed to Southend for use on the X1. (AS)

With RN being the registration code for Preston, you might hazard a guess that Highland Scottish Tiger E1 (PRN 125X) had a previous life before going north of the border, and you'd be right! New to Duple as a demonstrator, it was fitted with a scrolling dot matrix destination display – unusual for a coach. As can be seen in this view where it is parked at the back of Edinburgh's St Andrew's bus station, the dot matrix system was replaced with (I'm assuming) a conventional roller blind. (AS)

When the NBC joined forces with Trathens and expanded the Rapide network, they didn't have enough suitable coaches, so several Leopards, including National Travel West's 81 (SND 281X), were upgraded. This included the fitment of a toilet, servery and roof-mounted pod to house the screen to watch the obligatory in-journey video. Whilst the steel sprung Leopard wasn't really a match for what Devon's finest was putting out, they were reputed to be rather rapid and did the job until something more suitable came along – more on that later. (AS)

A nice splash of colour to brighten things up! South Wales Transport's Leopard 115 (MKH 678A), originally registered MCY115X. One of six similar coaches delivered to SWT in 1982 originally for National Express work, they later migrated to the company's coaching unit and when SWT formed United Welsh Coaches based at Gorseinon, they transferred there. SWT seemed to have a thing about these MKH/A plates as most of the coach fleet seems to have carried one at some point. (AS)

The slightly narrower front axle indicates that all is not quite as it seems. In 1975, Greater Manchester PTE took delivery of twelve ECW-bodied Leopards. After a few years they showed signs of rot, so in 1982 seven were sent to Duple for rebodying, emerging as 82-8 (SND 82-8X). In 1987, three were acquired by Chester, and 22 (SND 87X) is seen in the company's depot. The cobbles and tram lines were still there when First acquired Chester in 2007 and I was sent to give the place the once-over; I don't think the depot had changed since this photograph was taken. (AS)

Sweeping round Parliament Square is Wallace Arnold's only Dominant IV which, unusually, was bought second-hand. New in 1982 and bought by WA from Hutchison of Overtown in 1985, Volvo B10M FGD 826X was allocated to the Devon fleet. It arrived at the same time as five new Berkhof Esprit-bodied B10Ms which carried DSV 708-12, so this received DSV 721 from the same run. (AS)

In the back of my mind I've got this notion that when operators other than NBC subsidiaries were permitted to tender for National Express contracts, Lincoln City Transport were one of the first to succeed. Either way, here's a really polite Lincoln coach on National Express work. Seen on layover in London, Tiger PYE 838Y was new to Grey-Green in 1983, passing to Lincoln four years later. (AS)

Above and below: The largest batch of SBG-fronted Dominants went not to an SBG operator but to London Country for use on a variety of work including Green Line, National Express and the airport-link services. Forty-five were delivered and again were leased from Kirkby on a five-year deal, classified as TD (Tiger/Duple). Fresh from a repaint into the rather attractive later all-over green livery, TD 5 (YPD 105Y) is seen travelling down Buckingham Palace Road whilst National Holidays-liveried TD33 (YPD 133Y) crosses Kingston Bridge on a National Express working. (AS)

It wasn't common for operators to specify the Dominant IV with chrome side trim, especially cost-conscious NBC subsidiaries, but Oxford South Midland did just that on the ten-strong EBW batch of Tigers. When privatisation saw the company split in two, several of the batch went to the newly formed South Midland company, which was later taken over by Transit Holdings, who then launched the Oxford Tube to compete against the established Oxford Citylink services. The first of the batch EBW 101Y, named New College, is seen on Oxford High Street heading for the capital. (AS)

It's a good job there's not one of those full-width spray suppressors fastened to the back of Glover of Ashbourne's Tiger YNN 396Y. Seen in London in 1992, it had done well to keep its tiger's head radiator badge for all those years as they had a habit of 'falling off'. (PG)

The year 1982 saw six brand-new vehicles enter the fleet of Thomson's of Trentham, three of them being Dominant-bodied Fords. By this time the Thomson family had relinquished ownership of the company and it wasn't to be too much longer before it was then sold to Copeland's of Meir. Ford R1114 YRF 752Y is seen arriving at Wembley. (AS)

A nice bit of bus racing going on: Dominant vs Paramount. It's good to see the driver of Merseybus' Tiger 7016 (EKA 216Y) getting into the spirit of things by wearing a St Helens top. The location: Wembley. The date: 27 April 1991. The event: Wigan vs St Helens in the Rugby League Challenge Cup Final. This was definitely on the way to the match, as St Helens lost 13-8. (AS)

Here we see the opposite end of the Tricentrol chassis conversion range, CVH 732Y, an 8-metre-long Ford T152. New to Abbeyway's in 1983, when just over a year old it joined South Yorkshire PTE's Coachline division. Fitted with back-to-back seats around tables and a Dominant II front bumper, it is seen in SYPTE's Doncaster depot. (AS)

As the Dominant's successors, the Laser and Caribbean had been in production for nearly two years, and the Leopard's successor, the Tiger, for longer than that, there has to be a story behind Dix of Dagenham's Leopard A848 VML. New in 1979 to Skill's of Nottingham as FRA 64V, its Plaxton Supreme body was burnt out in 1982, following which the Cowie Group acquired the chassis and had it rebodied. (AS)

A459 FHH was the only Tiger operated by Yeowart's of Whitehaven and was notable in being the final Dominant-bodied 11-metre Tiger to enter service. It passed to Cumberland Motor Services in 1988 when they acquired the Yeowart's business, then moved within the Stagecoach empire to Stagecoach East Midland's coaching unit, Rainworth Travel. (AS)

Goldliner

After being used on the aborted Bedford concept project back in 1975, Duple reincarnated the Goldliner name in 1980 for 126 high-floor bodies built on the Volvo B10M, Leyland Tiger and Dennis Falcon V chassis. The Goldliner body was approximately a foot higher than a standard Dominant, with fourteen of them featuring a standard-height front end (with the narrow bumper as per the Dominant III and IV), which then stepped up approximately a foot immediately behind the entrance door. The rest of the Goldliners did away with the stepped effect by having the area above the entrance door mould into the roofline by way of either an illuminated name panel, or in most cases a destination box. In a turn-about from their normal-height counterparts, there were more Goldliner IIIs built than Goldliner II or IVs (fifty-five IIIs vs twenty-two IIs and forty-nine IVs), with all but five of the Goldliner IIIs delivered to Scottish operators. Mention must be made here of the ten Goldliner IV-bodied Dennis Falcon Vs, built – at very short notice – for the NBC to operate their newly introduced Rapide services. Designated as the Super Goldliner, they were fitted with comfortable reclining seats, onboard food and drink servery, toilet, video, and entertainment systems and powered by a 260bhp rear-mounted turbocharged Perkins V8 engine, they truly were magnificent machines. The chassis were designed, built, and delivered to Duple in a ridiculously short space of time and the completed vehicles were ready to hit the road just over twelve months after the concept was agreed. The rushed production and lack of practical development time soon became apparent when the coaches started to spectacularly fail and, in some cases, self-combust, and no further orders were made.

The Goldliner made its debut in 1981, with the rarest variant being the Goldliner II, of which only twenty-two were produced. Originally delivered as a Duple demonstrator, Volvo B10M CNS 549X then passed to Les Bywater of Rochdale where it was used on the company's daily service to London, where it is seen parked in London Gloucester Road coach station. (AS)

The Goldliner II and IV differed only by the size of their standard-shaped side windows but the stepped roofline is clearly visible. Happy Days of Woodseaves ordered three Goldliner II-bodied Volvo B10Ms in 1982, with 146 (WVT 887X) seen here taking part in the 1982 Brighton coach rally. It was later rebodied with a Macedonian-built MCCI body. (AS)

Another Goldliner II operator was Coliseum of Southampton, who ordered two, including fifty-seven-seat JBK 111X. Bearing in mind the Goldliner was a premium coach body and the two would have been the pride of Coliseum's fleet, it seems odd to have had one of them fitted with the maximum number of seats. (AS)

Above and below: The largest order for Goldliners went to Park's of Hamilton, the order for forty on Volvo B10Ms making not only the headlines in the trade press at the time but also being used by Duple to good effect through several publicity campaigns. As was usual for Park's, they carried the liveries of several tour companies, as seen on FHS 742 and 746X, both parked in Argyle Street, London. (AS)

The Park's order contained Goldliner III and IVs, although I'm not sure how happy some of the tourists would be trying to see past one of those wide window pillars on the Goldliner III. Aero Tours of Lincoln, a subsidiary of Wilby's of Hibaldstow, operated FHS 760X, which had previously been with fellow Lincolnshire operator Sleafordian, where it received the Lincolnshire reg FTL 728X. (RS)

Little things such as the Manchester registration 'Go In Style' on the dome, air horns and mascot on the roof indicate that at one time Delta Coaches' XVU 917X had been part of my mate Wesley's Go Goodwin's fleet, and indeed it was his grandad Alan's first executive coach. New as FHS 726X, I've seen photos of the coach taken a good five years after it left Goodwin's and that mascot was still safely fixed to the coach. (RS)

The Goldliners only lasted about two years at Park's and were soon spread far and wide. FHS 745X almost reached the opposite end of the British Isles when purchased by Hookway's of Devon. Several owners later, it returned to Devon with Taw & Torridge where it became NDO 856. I remember this particular motor did quite a lot of National Express duplication work, and it is doing just that when seen at Taunton in 1992. (PG)

Another Goldliner I remember from National Express duplicates was Tiger JXI 9141, new as BLH 717Y to Hamilton of Uxbridge. Their location meant they were the operator of first resort whenever a last-minute 'dupe' was needed from VCS or Heathrow. JXI was even painted into National Express livery – an indication of how often they were used. It was unique amongst the Goldliner IIIs as not only was it the only Tiger not delivered new to the SBG, it was also the only one with a stepped roofline. Not wanting to be left out however, it did make its way to Scotland, becoming one of the first coaches bought by Andy McCall of Lockerbie. (RS)

Above and below: In 1982, Grey-Green purchased Goldliner IV-bodied Tigers with a mix of manual and semi-automatic gearboxes. All six migrated to South Wales operators: one to Parfitt of Rhymney Bridge and five to South Wales Transport. These later transferred to fellow Badgerline Group companies: three to Western National and two to Badgerline itself. At SWT, the five received registrations all beginning with FDZ 98 and, as two of the WN ones had the same fleet numbers as the Badgerline two, you had to make sure you got the right coach if they were ever parked up together. Seen with Grey-Green when fairly new is OHM 832Y, whilst Badgerline's 2201 (FDZ 981, formerly OHM 835Y) is seen departing Chippenham with one of the company's Van Hool-bodied Volvos giving chase. Having driven all the WN ones, I can remember that the semi-auto one really struggled to pull away, having only the 218bhp TL11 engine and the heavy Goldliner body. (AS/RS)

Not many NBC fleets purchased Goldliners new – only National Travel (East) had more than a handful. With the driver making sure his tie is straight for the photograph, National Holidays-liveried OHE 264X is seen at Scratchwood Services (now London Gateway) on the M1 in 1986. A Goldliner II, note the full-length offside Continental door. (AS)

Seen travelling down East Parade in Rhyl is a motor that managed to spend all its fleet life in Wales and Scotland. RJI 4378 was new as RSJ 812Y to Volvo in Irvine as a demonstrator (those of a certain age will remember it appearing on the cover of *Buses* magazine in 1982). It was then acquired by Caelloi Motors of Pwllheli and then, as seen here, M&H of Dinbych. It then joined forces with JXI 9141 with Andy McCall in Lockerbie before ending its days with MacEwan of Anisfield. (RS)

Above and below: Remember earlier I said the Dominant IV-bodied Leopards were only a stop-gap on Rapide work? Well, here are the monsters they were filling in for. I've gone into detail about the story behind the ten Dennis Falcon Vs delivered to the NBC and their subsequent disastrous careers in the main text, so here's a few shots of them in action. A direct replacement for one of the Leopards was National Travel West's 99 (ANA 99Y), seen flying down the M1 near Kings Langley in Hertfordshire in 1983. Having arrived at VCS, we see a candidate for the most fleet names on one coach! Five of the ten went to Western National to provide their share of the West Country Rapide services operated jointly with Trathens. Exeter-based coaches carried the Greenslades name, and 2350 (AOD 643Y) appears to be heading well off its usual path, with Stranraer shown as its destination. (AS)

The remaining Falcon Vs that didn't meet a premature end by self-combusting were withdrawn by the NBC after only two years' service, but soon found new owners (some of whom used the coaches on National Express duplication work). Allowing a comparison in heights between a standard Dominant IV and the Goldliner, AOD 645Y looks in fine condition when operated by Albert Ripon Coaches of Long Eaton. (RS)

The end (literally) of the end. Believed to be the longest surviving Falcon V was former Western National AOD 644Y. It ended its operational life with Rooney's Coaches of Hilltown in County Down and finally met its end in 2006. There's not much room to access to the mighty Perkins V8, and overheating within the engine compartment with fuel leaking onto the engine being the causes of most of the burn-outs these vehicles suffered. (PG)

An indication of the popularity of long-distance coach travel in the latter part of the 1900s, not only has Scottish Citylink's 822 from Eastbourne to Edinburgh got two Duples of its own on it, there's also another one on the dupe tucked in behind that looks like it too is going north of the border. Fife Scottish Tiger FLT1 (SFS 581Y) was one of three similar coaches delivered in 1982, and as all the SBG Goldliners were originally Goldliner IIIs, then the middle coach had already had its rebuild to the standard window line. (AS)

Still in the original Citylink blue and white saltire livery, we see Western's Volvo B10M V150 (TSD 150Y) swinging off Buckingham Palace Road to access 'Sammy's', the arrivals area of VCS. It was so named as it was once the depot of Samuelson's New Transport. I'm sure many people using its affectionate name today will not know why. (AS)

I hope that bloke above FWH 23Y wasn't actually going to throw something onto Charterplan's Tiger FWH 23Y. One of three Tigers to join Greater Manchester Transport's coaching fleets in 1982 (two for Charterplan and one for Warburton's), they later received National Express livery and became the regular performers on the 825 Manchester to Gatwick service, where no doubt the drivers appreciated the extra luggage space the underfloor lockers provided. (AS)

Staying with the PTEs, we see West Yorkshire's Tiger 1602 (CUB 602Y). Like the coach from the right side of the Pennines seen above, it too went on to receive National Express livery as well as having roller blinds retrofitted into the destination box. It was caught backing off the stand at Sheffield's Pond Street bus station with Park Hill estate on the horizon. (RS)

Predominantly Dominants

As usual, I've rounded off the book with a selection of photographs with pairs (or more) of the subject matter, so I hope you enjoy these final examples of when Duple was dominant.

I've no idea where it is or what the occasion was, but it's just such an evocative 1970s street scene full of British motor engineering with just a hint of things to come – a Portuguese Caetano-bodied coach on the left and what looks like a Toyota Celica on the right, ready to do muscle-car battle with the Mk 1 Capri. Three Leopards from National's Cheltenham-based Black & White fleet take centre stage. (AS)

Mention was made earlier about the Margo family, and here we see another offshoot. Plaskow and Margo were both nephews of the founder of Margo's of Bexleyheath and ran coaches under various permutations of the Atlas name (as can be seen here) and later went on to operate tendered services in London under the Atlas Bus name. Seen in Eastbourne are Bedford YRT ONK 867L and Leopard JRO 387L, both new to the company. (AS)

Midland General 76 and 77 (XRC 605/6M), a pair of 1974 Bedford YRQs await their tour customers outside the York House Hotel on Royal Parade, Eastbourne, when brand new. Judging by the passengers wearing their big coats and headscarves, they were obviously experiencing typical British seaside weather. The driver seems to have the luxury version of the 'extra step' – no upturned milk crate for his passengers! (AS)

Another pair of lightweight National whites, this time a pair of Ford R114s from the Southdown fleet. There must have been a change in the weather as not only are the top sliders wide open, but there's plenty of bingo wings on display. (AS)

We've also seen plenty of ex-Fox of Hayes coaches, so how about two when they were still operating. YJH 704/6M were two members of a batch of no less than twenty Dominant-bodied Bedford YRTs delivered in 1975. Going by there also being a Golden Miller of Feltham coach to the right and the number in the window of YJH 704M, they were on a club outing to Eastbourne. (AS)

After their respective takeovers by Tyne & Wear PTE but before they were combined into Armstrong-Galley, the two constituents shared a common livery but carried their individual names as shown on Leopards 92 and 95 (GBB 992/5N). (AS)

I mentioned that most of the Nottingham 'Lilac Leopards' were sold to Maidstone, so here's proof I ain't a lyin. With GRC 884N carrying Maidstone's livery and 883/5 still retaining their lilac scheme, the latter two looking rather more dishevelled than their sister, the Maidstone Monarch. Interestingly GRC 884N has acquired a front destination dome since departing Nottingham as originally delivered, its front end was the same as its two counterparts. (AS)

Seen in Princes Park, Eastbourne, are two of the six Ford R1114s delivered to Hodge's of Sandhurst in 1978. The last Dominant I drove, a 1980 Bedford YMT, was collected one snowy January from Hodge's when the coach was approaching its fortieth birthday. I had low expectations as to its condition and wondered what state both the coach and I would be in when we arrived back in Stoke. I needn't have worried; Hodge's had looked after it so well that I can honestly say it was the nicest Bedford/Dominant combination I've ever driven. (AS)

Talking of Bedfords I've driven, I did a fair few miles in the one on the right when at Sanders of Holt. Part of the eighteen-strong batch of identical coaches delivered to Eastern National in 1978, Express-bodied BNO 695T was used by Bedford as part of a publicity campaign when new. (AS)

Whilst the Leopard was the standard NBC coach during the 1970s, Bedfords did feature in several fleets and were quite often ordered in conjunction with their heavier counterparts. National Travel (London) took thirty-one coaches in the BGY-T sequence in 1979, eighteen of them being on Bedford YMTs, including this fine pair seen in Eastbourne when new. (AS)

Just up the road from Hodge's was the chocolate-and-cream-coloured fleet of Reliance of Newbury, who for many years added two brand-new coaches to the fleet anually. Having just been delivered in April 1979, Ford R1114s 160/1 (YCF 966/7T) sit in the depot waiting for their first job. (AS)

Ebdon of Sidcup's 1979 order was for five 12-metre PSU5 Leopards: one with a Plaxton Supreme, the other four with Dominant IIs. Half of them are seen here, EBM 436/7T. (AS)

Those south-east NBC subsidiaries East Kent and Maidstone & District did like retrofitting those blue destination blinds, and I think it gave them an air of individuality. M&D Leopards CKR 155T and JKK 162V, both new to the company, are seen undertaking National Holidays feeder work. (AS)

As well as an extensive network of stage carriage services, Whippet of Fenstanton also ran several holiday express services for which their Volvo B58s were an ideal piece of kit. Eastbourne is the location again with the town's Grade II listed signal box in the background, and EAV 814V and an unidentified sibling prepare for the journey back to Cambridgeshire. (AS)

Many independent operators were grateful to the big tour fleets such as Shearings, Wallace Arnold and Smiths, who, replacing large numbers of vehicles on a regular basis, provided affordable but modern additions to smaller fleets. I remember one of my local operators in Cornwall in the 1980s raving about how good the two ex-Smiths Volvo/ Dominants they had purchased were. Forty TND-X Dominants made up Smiths 1982 order: ten Ford R1114s and thirty Volvo B58s, with three of the latter seen here. (AS)

...and another one comes to an end. The final picture in this journey through Duple's Dominant years sees half of the four Tigers delivered to Lothian in 1982. Late model Dominant IIs, Lothian's simple unadorned black and white livery shows how (provided it's kept clean) a coach can look elegant without having to be colourful. (AS)